THE WORLD IS OPEN TO THOSE WHO GIVE . . .

OTHER BOOKS BY GEORGE BETTS

Visions of You

Growing Together (with Donni Betts)

My Gift to You

Farewells Are Only Beginnings

George Betts

Tears and Pebbles in my Pockets

Photographs by
Maria Demarest
and
Michael Powers

CELESTIAL ARTS
Millbrae, California

First printing: February, 1976
Manufactured in the United States of America

4 5 6 7 8 9 10 11 12 — 82 81 80 79 78

Library of Congress Cataloging in Publication Data

Betts, George, 1944-
    Tears and pebbles in my pocket.

    I. Title.
PS3552.E85T4   811'.5'4   75-28752

Dedication . . .

for Viddie

My mind is wandering again,
    going its own directions.
I'm not afraid
                just to let it be . . .
It will flow
    and take me
        to new places,
            exciting ideas,
and feelings
        beyond my present understanding.
I will be richer . . .
My journey will build
        a bridge for my tomorrow.

People come and go,
   acquaintances are
         easily forgotten,
true friends are hard
         to come by.
Everything moves so fast . . .
I've known you
       for more than a year now.
I've learned your moods,
     felt your joys and sorrows
and shared your ever-changing
          approach to life.
You're spontaneous—
     acting rather than reacting,
loving rather than waiting to be loved
and giving while others hesitate.
You have learned to be yourself.
For this I admire and love you.
My world is more complete
     with you as my friend.

It's not the right time.
I can tell by the look
in your eyes . . .
you're afraid,
uncertain,
hesitant
but I understand.
I've been there.

At one time I was so afraid of rejection
that I waited three months
before saying hello . . .
eventually I learned how
but it's never easy.

I feel sorry for you . . .

You're limiting yourself
                and your world,
slowly drifting away from people,
        retreating safe within,
                where no one can reach you.

The farther you retreat,
        the harder it will be
                for you to come out.

I want to reach out
                and touch you,
        to let you know
                how much I care
but our words are often lost
                        when we argue.

I don't want to criticize . . .
only to love.

I'm writing again.
It feels good!
I can accept
      the dry times
but when the words return
          I feel refreshed,
as if I have a new dawn,
          a special time for me.

I wrote about you last night
but I'm afraid to share
the writing with you.

Could you accept it?
Would you reject me?

Right now it's too big a risk.
I hope someday I'll feel secure enough
to share it with you,
but as I write I realize
it will never happen unless
I take the risk today.

I seek in others
things I cannot
find in you.

Sometimes it's a smile,
        a soft word
                or a warm caress
and other times
                it's nothing,
for you have met my needs.

Time travels on,
        I change,
                so do you . . .

Let us both never forget
that nothing is the same forever,
that our love will experience
many different moods
                        but it will continue . . .

I have been limiting myself,
    my creativity,
by not slowing down
        and taking time
to allow things to flow . . .
I've known this
      for so long
but sometimes it's so hard
to relearn or remember.

I stand in front,
confident and self-assured,
facilitating the class
and the topics being discussed,
but there's a different me
                    you don't know.
I also sit at a desk
        deep within the role of a student.
Usually I achieve my goals
        but sometimes I fall short
and I worry just like you.
I wonder what you would think if
        you could see me when I fail.

The first day
     we met
     we knew
         we had something special,
something that didn't
       need to be defined.
It was a feeling . . .
     closeness,
         caring,
             even love.
It began silently
       and has grown ever since . . .

I have given
but have not
received because
I do not know
how to ask
for what I need.

We are safe!
The lights were so dim,
the smoke so thick
and the music so loud
that there was no way
for us to communicate.

I hurt inside
when I see you
trying so hard,
gathering people
around you,
planning activities,
continually trying
to impress,
asking the proper
questions, and
stating the correct
responses.

Your insecurity shows
to almost everyone,
everyone but you.

Go ahead and cry . . .
Please don't hold back
because of me.

Your tears will
cleanse your soul,
allowing you to
release those emotions inside.

I only wish I had been told
it was okay to cry as a child
instead of being taught that
"big boys don't cry!"

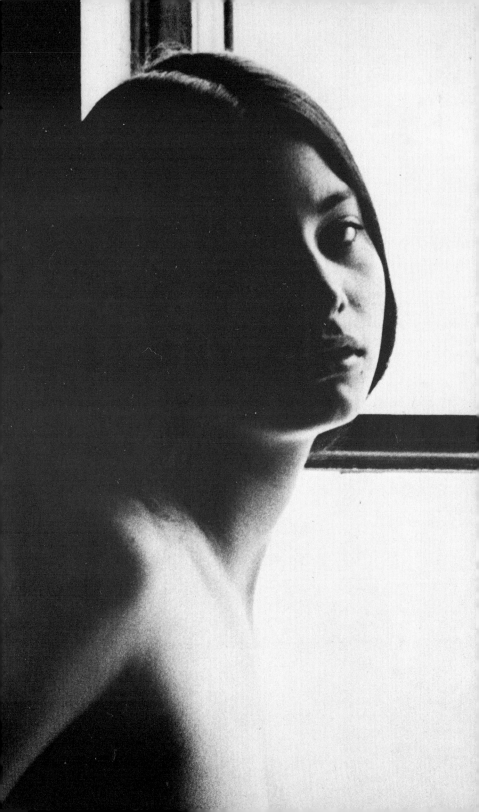

I'm sitting in my car
    in the middle of nowhere,
        with no place to go,
            no place to stay.

I have stopped,
    here,
        alone,
afraid,
    confused.

Alone with my struggles,
I have nowhere to go.

Tonight I'm lost,
    but with the dawn,
I will begin once again . . .

Time heals some things
but for others it becomes
a reminder of unfinished conflicts.

We were so close,
sharing secrets and
        living dreams
but for unknown reasons
we drifted apart.

I was never happy with this,
nor did I know what to do,
        what to say,
but you finally found the courage
I could not find and asked me
what was wrong.

Now we know how important
it is to be truthful,
how damaging it can be
        if we aren't,
and how rewarding it is when
                we are.

Our friendship has known conflict
and because of this, both of us
have grown.

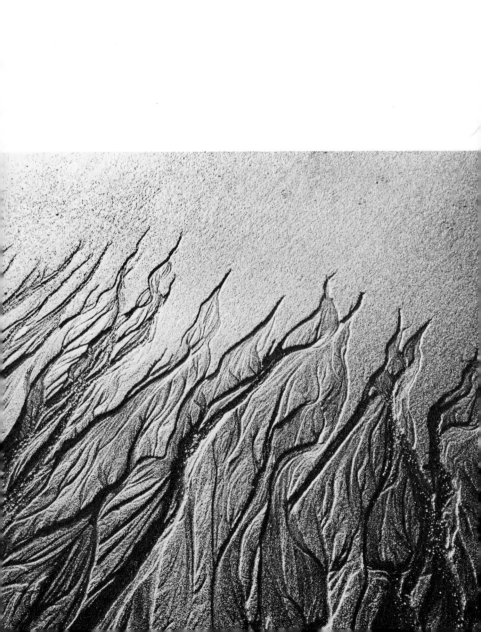

I cried for me last night.
I had lost something inside.
My journey began with confusion
and traveled through anger and sorrow
until I reached my place of understanding.

Sometimes I lose you in the clouds.
I search for other people
and become so involved
that I forget
        that your beauty,
                your being,
                        your sensual feelings,
nurture me to be sensitive
and understanding.
What you are, totally,
        helps me so much
                to be what I am,
what I strive to be,
        and what I am becoming . . .

Being with other people
helps me appreciate you.

Because we
    continue to
        change,
we continue
    to be . . .

The more I see you
the deeper my admiration grows,
for you are becoming a beautiful person.
You are growing in so many ways
but what I admire most is your ability
to show your emotions, to let
others know how much you care.

You have a gift of love . . .
There is such beauty
          in your giving.

To meet your needs
I sacrificed my own
which left me unsatisfied,
unable to continue
and confused as to what
                    I wanted to do.
What would be best?
        Leave frustrated,
                begin once more,
                        or choose to do nothing?

My mind and heart remained separated,
                        so did we.
I wanted to settle this
and find us together once more,
but somehow neither of us
                        knew the way.

I'm alone now . . .
music softly playing,
guitars and Spain,
a lullaby of sadness . . .

The sun is leaving
        for another day . . .
I'm drifting,
        yesterday,
                today,
but not yet
        tomorrow . . .

I'm alone now . . .
        the music,
                my reminder,
my lullaby of sadness.

I know you
          almost
as well as
          I know me.
I have learned
          your moods,
     your expressions,
your ability to give
          and receive,
and the way you strive
to be . . .

Your past
          holds both joy
                    and sorrow
               and your future
                    is becoming
                              brighter
          for you are developing
                              you.

I smile silently
          as you continue to grow . . .

I cried for you tonight.
Not because of what you are,
but because of what is
                    happening to you.

You are a brilliant man
but time is consuming
your hourglass of life.

Your years are passing,
            your hair is turning gray
and I find it hard to
                accept the changes.

I want to protect you,
            to slow you down,
                to erase your confusion,
to restore your beautiful mind
but I am limited.
                        I cannot make things
easier for you,
            or for me.
I can only listen and care,
            and hold you when you cry.

I miss you.
I have now for many months
although you are so near.
I see and hear you
but I do not understand you.

You have your needs
and I have mine.
I work at mine
while you work at yours
and we remain so unaware
of each other.

This leaves us both
isolated and alone.
I have limited myself
by seeing only me
and you have done the same.

What more do we need
to become aware of each other?

Does a person ever reach
a place of total contentment?
Will I ever be satisfied
with what I am at the moment
or will I continue to want more?

Life has been good for me.
I have most everything I need
but I still want more.
What will I find when
                    I look within?
What will I do when
everyone has left
and I am alone?

Will I follow the tragedy of many
        or find the strength of few?
Can I accept change?
                    within me?
                        within you?
or will I fight and resist?

The wind is blowing gently outside.
I hear the windchime,
        bringing music to my world.
Can I listen?
            Do I hear?
                Who am I?

Your travels are beginning once again,
    to a faraway land
        filled with new adventures,
    excitement
        and the opportunity to grow.

Your journey will be successful
    for you have the courage,
        the desire
      and the ability
to discover beauty around you
        and within you.

I send you on your way
    with my love . . .

Passing seasons,
  many years,
    joy and laughter,
      tears and sorrow
and through it all,
  we remain together
    in our hearts.

Can you hear me?
There are so many
things inside
I need to say . . .

I need you to listen,
to hear beyond my words,
to sense my message inside.

A brilliant man once wrote
about how necessary it is
to have someone who cares,
          who takes time,
                    who listens,
but no one heard this man,
          only his concern for others,
and he took his life.

We can learn from him,
but only if we listen . . .

I tried tonight
but I could not
erase you from my mind.
For some unknown reason
I continue to think of you.

You're so young and beautiful.
The world is yours
        when you find yourself.

Your searching has led you to me
and for moments we will share deeply
but I know someday you'll move on
with my love as a part of you . . .

The road has been rocky,
with stumbling stones . . .
        competition,
                frustration,
                        failure.
I traveled alone most of the time.
I enjoyed and thrived on this
but there were times
        when I became lonely.

I finally realized that companionship
and love could enrich my life,
helping me to be more complete.

A sunset,
        a candlelit room,
                        soft music
are so much more
                now
with you.

I can't relax today,
     so much to do,
         so much to accomplish!

Why?
   to prove myself?

Why must I always
       be doing something?
I know I'd rather be walking
slowly through the park,
but here I sit and worry
about all that needs to be done.

Outside my window,
a young couple just
arrived at the park.
They seem so happy,
    giggling,
        playing,
as if they have a secret
and no one will ever find out.
I watch them hug
    as the phone rings
and I begin to prove
    myself once again . . .

It's been many years . . .
　　　　How have you changed?
Your voice sounded the same
　　　　　　over the phone,
but what about you,
　　　　　inside?

You were young and beautiful,
so in love with life,
　　living both the joys
　　　　　　and sorrows,
completely involved
　　　　with everything around you.

I'm anxious to see you again.
I need to have you know me now,
to rekindle our friendship,
to find out if memories last,
to know once again who you are.

Ideas are sometimes hazy in my head.
I want to express them
but the words cannot be found.

I want to express myself . . .
            to let you know where I am
but the words are lost inside.

Does my face show you
            that I need to be loved?

Morning
                    dawn
          no traffic
       birds singing
                    the silent sun
today
          slowly drifting upon us.

I'm content now
          no tension
                    no movement . . .
just appreciation
          for being alive.

If I hurt you,
    if I cause you pain,
please let me know.
Tell me, so we can work
        through our conflict.

I know it'll be hard,
        that it's a risk,
but if you don't tell me
and hold it inside,
    slowly we'll be destroyed.

All I can promise you
    is that I'll try to do the same,
                I'll tell you.

Last night
   while thinking
         about my life,
I thought about you
   and discovered
         a beautiful thing . . .

I love you!

This is something
I never realized before.
I have a deep appreciation
      from watching you
            live your life . . .

I want you to know
      that you're special,
            that I care.
My life is richer
      because of you.

You returned to the ocean today,
        not your beach,
                but one that woke
memories within you.

Memories which took you back . . .
You talked with him
            and shared silently
for you knew he would enjoy
        the elegance of the rocky shores
and the majestic feeling of the ocean.

For moments you left today
and reexperienced yesterday.
I watched in silence
for I didn't know what to say . . .

"Take Time To Enjoy"
the poster reads and
I silently agree as
I hurry to my next
appointment, already
thinking about tomorrow . . .

If I continue to talk,
someday you may choose to listen . . .

If I continue to listen,
someday you may allow me
to know who you are.

Tomorrow is your future
but today . . .
You must decide
      what to do . . .
It's such a risk,
knowing you might gain everything
                         or lose . . .

Somewhere,
    deep inside,
you possess the strength
      to decide what is best.
I know the struggle
         will be difficult
but there's no doubt
         in my mind,
you will succeed
and create
      your own happiness . . .

I sometimes find it difficult
to write about the good times,
            the times without
                        struggle or conflict,
the times without searching,
        the times when I'm at peace
                    with the world and myself.

These are the times I strive for,
but the times that are hardest to express.

Today I took time to write
while I'm happy,
                flowing,
                            content . . .
Tomorrow this feeling
                may float away
and my search may begin once more
but for today
        please share with me in my joy.

Your life is open
   for you have learned
to take time
         to understand . . .
      the flower,
         the sunrise,
      the serenity
        of a walk
           through the forest,
               alone.

Looking ahead
      to your tomorrow,
I see a world of love,
      a world of giving,
a world created
      for you,
        by you . . .

I'm sitting here
                doing nothing
but just feeling
                good about me.
It's a beautiful feeling
                doing nothing
just feeling good about me.
I'm smiling . . .

I'm a night person.
I come alive
      when others prepare
               for sleep.
I enjoy the darkness,
    the silence,
        the time for me
to reflect and ponder . . .

My creativity blossoms,
I become excited.
It's my time of day,
    when others sleep
and I build
    quietly through the night.

I close my eyes
        my body begins to relax
            taking me deeper
                to a pleasant state
no tension
        relaxation
where thoughts flow . . .

My mind becomes a wanderer.
I experience
            memories and dreams
pleasant thoughts
                plans for the future
my body is relaxed . . .
I feel good
        my mind is at peace
flowing . . .
                warm . . .

It's time to leave . . .
Our beginning is
coming to a close
and so we look
toward tomorrow . . .

But let's look at
yesterday and today.
We arrived here alone
and began our adventure
together slowly,
                carefully,
not sure of what
was expected or sure
of what we wanted.

But during our time
we gave up our
loneliness and insecurities.

We gained new friends,
            confidence in ourselves
and a special feeling
            which cannot be defined
by words . . .
We leave so much stronger
for we have shared deeply.
I look at all of you and
smile . . .
            for you are my friends.

Working with thousands of people in the field of personal growth and self-expression through seminars and workshops, Dr. Betts has succeeded in awakening participants to a new understanding and awareness of their natural surroundings. He is Adjunct Professor at the University of Northern Colorado, and Director of Alternative and Experiential Education at Arvada West High School in Jefferson County, Colorado.

George Betts (Ed.D.) is also author of the best-selling *VISIONS OF YOU* and *MY GIFT TO YOU*, and co-author, with Donni Betts, of *GROWING TOGETHER*.